The Mammoth Sunflower

Benjamin Jensen

Copyright © 2025 by Benjamin Jensen

All rights reserved, including the right to reproduce this book, or portions thereof, in any form. No part of this book may be used or reproduced in any manner whatsoever without written permission from the publisher, except in the case of brief quotations embodied in critical articles and reviews. The views expressed herein are the responsibility of the author and do not necessarily represent the position of the publisher. For information or permission, contact Benjamin via themammothsunflower@gmail.com.

These excerpts are part of a forthcoming work and may not be reproduced, distributed, or transmitted in any form without the author's prior written consent. Your support of the author's rights is appreciated.

Cover design by Ash Amos, Penrose Artist Co. 2024, www.ashamos.art
Sketch Illustration by Lem Ball, Instagram @lemonzestart
Interior print design and layout by Marny K. Parkin

Published by September Sunflowers

Paperback ISBN: 979-8-218-67943-9

A Prelude to
Heaven in Earth

Coming Soon

To the Sincere Individuals in an honest pursuit toward truth

To my brother Wesley

And, of course, to the Mammoth Sunflower

Prelude

Take hold of these leaves, whichever bring you lowest, then bloom your bloom—not mine, not another's. For what is theirs can never fully be yours nor what is yours ever to be fully theirs. Neither of us leading the one or the other; rather our endless unfurling leaves teaching each other home as we heal from that upward cycle of allowing leadership to pollute our teachings.

From the moment this plant sprouts, the initial wispy frame begins to face the sun, boldly claiming a place in the world—if permitted to grow old enough. And for those that do:

The days begin by praising eastward in the morning, following the sun rays through the afternoon then worshiping westward in the evening to conclude each day. Sundown, night's time and with it a faithful nightly reset to face east once again. This plant sways its frame for both good morning and good night, no matter the conditions. Even on cloudy days the Mammoth Sunflower faces where the Sun would be.

In an equal effort, if not more, that this flower devotes toward an upward spire, an eventual devotion toward an inward turn, a falling in love or in other words, a return to itself occurs. Up, up, and away until then and an incredible height for a flower is reached. That pursuit toward the Sun, an effort honored many times over by various unfurling leaves, eventually brings this plant to the point of an inevitable neglection—reaching toward the heavens while celestial beauties lie beneath. Celestial beauties that command attention yet who lay farther below. This flower's bloom remains hidden during this upward cycle and that frame I have spoken of casts a growing shadow on the garden and its variety. Until, the upward cycle is broken and a different fixation emerges, drastically introducing a frightening yet budding change of course.

After devoting an entire life and all efforts toward facing the Sun, this flower constructs a choice of nothing less than for survival. Eventually, this flower fully blooms. Heliotropic praises cease, and this newfound bloom begins to grow damningly downward toward Heaven, its life now becomes one great daring return. The previous swaying efforts, everything that its frame knew having nothing else left that it could have offered and up until this point unfamiliar with any other direction it could face. Such conditions make the daring act of the Mammoth Sunflower's return even more remarkable—a Divine display that no matter how devoted this was never too far up to be able to change. Compelled rather to return to the Earth, becoming its largest at its lowest point. A downward growth toward fellow celestial beauties once again, to its Heaven in Earth.

Could this bloom's upward spire have reached the Sun through those previous sways? Perhaps, though this chose not to find solace in doing so at the cost of future generations. This Mammoth Sunflower demonstrates the power of a fixation. When fixated toward the Sun, nearly becomes one itself in appearance. On the contrary, when the fixation of this bloom's worship changes toward the Earth, so to the transformation of its appearance and purpose from the previous to a reflection of the Earth: a bloom populating itself with potential life across a growingly spherical form. Whose seeds once developed most often display an off-white that appears painted as if it were with a blade of grass dipped in blackish ink then striped down their shells quite precisely and in as individual of a manner known to Nature, writing in Her own language upon their doorways that the potential for life now lies within. These seeds are then prepared, community'd together while yet their own, composing themselves like stars condensed within swirling spiral arms of a galaxy. When winds now shake this flower's frame, these seeds respond by falling to the Earth in their own time and way. Upon witnessing such a celestial event one could wonder if they have seen the stars of heaven fall to the Earth.

All of this, a result of a not-so-risky choice to break an upward Armageddon'd cycle. Now joining with fellow celestial beauties who in their movements to life's winds seem to rustle the tune that if one thinks they are unworthy or worthy, they are correct—a natural demonstration of that endowed right, by simply existing. So now this final shift to face what matters most, the Earth—even as the Sun does.

The Mammoth Sunflower remains well into the latter part of the year before its wedding with the Earth. Its bowed frame remains in the garden like a towering monument and appears as if it were Nature's Tower of Babel. Whose purpose grew to be the opposite, uniting what others claim the previous to have separated. A celestial demonstration that Nature knows no limits in the ability to heal that of Her's which becomes polluted. For unlike the biblical tower, this tower possesses the potential to lower any who, if willing, feels the motives of its life engraved along its base. If one's eyes—seemingly inevitably—wander upward after happening upon the base of this sacred giant, they are brought down once again, this time even lower, by the gaze of that crowned final bow. These are those who see what this flower saw—never to be forgotten by anyone who does. These are those who see that the Earth would take upon Herself the consequence of becoming pillars of salt rather than to suffer without the Mammoth Sunflower's final gaze, so She may not lie alone among the destruction. Rejoicing then at this return as She sends forth all of September's Sunflowers with their sporadic petaly praises to illuminate these hazy conditions.

A love story of a flower, destined toward reaching the Sun but who looks back instead. That downward choice propelling it much further than an upward spire ever could have. Now liberated through an inward turn, it hopes the Earth's soil will receive an individually prepared future generation who year after year can use the same power to break all cyclic remains, those who can wander on their own unique journeys, finding additional power not in always having faced the same direction but in being able to change, no matter the conditions.

The yearly emphasis on preparing the next generation is perhaps one of the most grounding characteristics of this deity and resonates further sentiments throughout our environments that the quality of a generation is not so much based upon its achievements alone but more so on the achievements of the next. This Mammoth Sunflower, experiencing many changes throughout its life's journey all the while never having actually changed itself, rather having become more of itself.

Oh, Mammoth Sunflower, you may have persuaded me with this year's final bow, you do seem a lot like a Sincere Individual.

I have heard that if you watch the Mammoth Sunflower grow for long enough, you might just find your way home too, eventually.

The Mammoth Sunflower

A simple seed,

roots sinking

from the dirt

freed.

*An innocence that could
make one giggle.*

Where Heaven met me.

Sunlight hits

leafy frame;

Mammoth Sunflower,

turns away?

*I will not turn
my face from you,
I will follow you.*

Facing,

no matter how

the day.

Deepens in soil,

wispy frame

soar higher!

*Here's my frame
here's my everything.*

        The days pass
        faithfully pass.
        Heliotropic praises.

Sun shining,
beautiful days but

                          ugly on the inside,
                          that's okay.

        Cloudy days, warmth
        not felt.

Clouds looming,
ugly days but

                          beautiful on the inside,
                          that's okay.

        Even on cloudy days,
        where the Sun would,
        so this is.

The light
never hides,
after all.

        East in the morning
        west in the evening
        Sunsets.
        Night's darkness
        turning still
        east again.

*And then I'll wake up
and I'll wait,
for you.*

No gates,
No earning,
Sunrises.

Again,

*Each hello
a new opportunity
for better goodbyes.*

again,

*Whatever shows our love
the most
is true doctrine.*

and again.

*A light that fills
the gaps of love,
not the gaps of fear.*

And again.

*If all we have known
should flee us,*

*a love for ourselves,
for each other,
can still remain.*

The Sun
the Mammoth Sunflower
faces.

*Unceasingly enough
no matter
the sways.*

A journey

to reach

the heavens

while

Celestial beauties

lie beneath.

Told to lose myself and
get to work

　　　　　　　　　before having had the chance

　　　　　　　　　　　　to find myself.

Up, up,

away.

I deserve better
than this desire
to be favored.

Grows,

only grows.

Led to think I could never
be enough

　　　　　　　　　so I learned to do

　　　　　　　　　　　too much.

Shadows cast on those

once nearest.

Until,

*They had me promise
I could be like you, and
I believe them.*

                                              *But now I see
I must be
all of me.*

                   Bloom

                      fully blooms.

                 Heliotropic praises,

                          cease.

I paid a debt I did not owe.

                                    *Afraid of rejection
yet I reject myself.*

*So now I leave the 99
and return to the 1.*

                    Same frame

                 different direction.

*The fears of tomorrow
cannot keep me
from the me of today.*

                             *If it cannot make me quit
I will not fear it.*

                  An inward turn,

*No one can
teach me anything*

                        *that my Soul is not capable
of teaching myself.*

               The Mammoth Sunflower

                        falls?

*I wish to enjoy
no good thing
or so-called blessing*

*I cannot adequately teach
anyone else to enjoy
for themselves.*

Not quite.

*I do not claim
to know many things,*

*but now I do know
when I don't know.*

Falling down,

further

down, toward

Heaven.

My Sincerity was Divinity.

*We were not gullible.
We were honest.*

That smiling

that mighty

the Mammoth

Sunflower,

now shows

a crowned, petalled bow.

*No amount of a God's love
can make any difference*

*if we are not first taught how
to properly love ourselves.*

The Earth

The Mammoth Sunflower faces—

Even as the Sun does.

*No longer governed
or damned by the old,
renewed by the now.*

                                        There doesn't have to be
                                                  an Armageddon;
                                                  the choice is ours.

                    All height

                        gone.

*I had to lose my mind,
your mind,
before I could find it.*

                    Grows

                    lower!

*Shamed away
from my natural self*

                                                and I wondered why
                                                      I was sick.

                    Until,

Heaven in Earth.

                                                        One
                                                        great
                                                  daring return.

                  No if-thens

                  Here, Now.

*A loving of ourselves,
together.*

                  Sunshine?

*While now I do not know
if truth exists,*

                                                  still I see
                                          that comfort does.

                    Still,

                      always.

Let me resign eternities for this, the renewal of our vows—to be buried in Heaven.
Who am I
to be united?
Then to be,

if only

for our moment,
the praises
illuminating these conditions.
No matter how I senesce
a contemplation upon the sacred,

this opportunity to return
to Her from whence, I sprang.
Not destined to be cast out
and forgotten

at the end of this life
by She.

No matter how I have lived
no matter what I have done
She considers me

to become one with Her.
This aspect of Nature,
banishing the polluted thoughts

that I could obtain a worthiness,
an upward heaven,
through my own merits
or understandings.
For if the essence of my existence
depends on more

than an acceptance;
a complete love
for my present self.

If I require extrinsic love,
no matter how pure,

no matter how well-intentioned,
to be complete,
then I never was,

then I never can be.
Then my worth,
a contradictory sway

to these extrinsic conditions.

> *To some my worst quality*
> *now that of no longer needing*
> *to be saved.*

Having discovered
the original,
this complete acceptance
> *of the Earth,*
> *of my Soul.*

A note before a symphony,

A radicle's emergence,

A story to end all stories,

> *But what say do I have in the matter?*
> *I am*

The Mammoth Sunflower

—Lem Ball, muralist and illustrator.

"... I beheld a seed as white as snow, which fell forth between the cracks of the hands of the sower and into the chasm of the Earth. And upon falling therein, began to feel the licks of the flames from the gates of despair. And upon feeling those licks, entering a sort a rage went further toward the source and smote off its tongue..."

". . . False summits and false horizons. Every time I think to have arrived at a knowledge, it eludes me . . ."

"... The Soul: the culmination of an Individual's thoughts filtered out and condensed by our greatest desires, liberated or damned by our action or inaction to participate in life's greatest wonder: the bringing of one's desires to life. Or greatest tragedy: to have never done so . . ."

"... When one better understands the past, the present is more easily understood. Understandable to feel on edge when led to believe the end is always near. The only true Armageddon is the acceptance of another's thoughts fully as one's own: a sold Soul. Yet to have no acquaintance and to speak each other's Sincere thoughts once left unsaid: the Divine entanglements of our Souls..."

"... The Soul decays under authority: an outward dependence on ever-changing fixations, on foreign spirits, to guide and direct—I have my own spirit, standing ready in its Sincerity! Requires no worthiness, dares not to leave me in my mistakes, not a whimsical voice misunderstood for my own nor an outward force acting mysteriously from within but the very core of an Individual, revealing itself: the desires nearest to the heart, most often unspoken..."

*"... The return of consciousness to the Individual ...
Let me show you how to sing forever ..."*

"... Sincerity ... the Divine force deeming one capable of all things that become near to the heart—things others may assume one to be incapable of, things in which that other is yourself, and especially things in which there looms the fear of falling short. For unlike that upward spire there is no falling short when falling in love, when falling downward toward Heaven, to ourselves..."

"... Capable of discovering more life purposes than lost with each passing day. Capable of devoting the loveliest affection toward any, no matter the size or reward. Capable, through a sort of rage, of considering oneself better than one's conditions and therefore, become so. Capable of discovering authority's greatest weakness: complete love and acceptance of oneself. Capable then of achieving this life's greatest victory: to stand unashamedly as oneself in any setting. Then, should time permit, capable of fulfilling the Sincerest purpose of all: to help others receive what they themselves once lacked. By doing so, believing one day this world will never know what it means to be without. None existing without purpose. For we all have lacked or cared for someone or something..."

". . . Our Sincere efforts are sufficient . . ."

"... You may think the universe is expanding away from us, but I tell you: The universe has turned to face us, has bloomed, and is now expanding through us. The potential for life now lies within..."

"... No institution can be large enough to contain us; none compassionate enough to sustain us. Even the universe itself may not be able to contain: the magnitude of the Sincere Individual. I believe in you. Capable of becoming limitless, populating across the universe forever until we become the stars of heaven who fall to the Earth. Once we turn inward to the Earth, to ourselves, we then can experience a love not yet fully realized: becoming true lovers of each other, not our own reflections in another..."

". . . Everyone must treat themselves with the rarity of which we are. There can never be too many of us; there have only been too many leaders and those who have lost themselves to leadership . . ."

". . . Imitation is the Sincerest form of slavery . . ."

"... Their sure knowledge of things impedes healing, for if one surely knows there is no more discovery. Knowledges cannot change or progress any further, but beliefs can. Should one ask how to be persuaded of the ludicrous of a knowledge, many times all it takes is the supposed knowledge to be stated back to them, at a future date..."

". . . That attempt to connect with an upward heaven, that neglection that severance of relationships with each other, with myself, persuades me therefore to unfurl these leaves, painful and bitter though it may be for some to see, there is a Heaven in Earth for you and for me. The daring choice to be taught by our love not led by our fears, the choice to look back no matter the conditions, if chosen:

*Our love becoming like September Sunflowers—
Everywhere I look I see you . . .*"

". . . Resurrected every time I cross your mind . . ."

". . . In perhaps the greatest of Nature's ironies: collectively as we fall downward, turn inward, toward Heaven, to ourselves, we become connected to each other. Our likeness found mainly in each becoming our own . . ."

". . . Yet how alike we all are. How alike those before us, hunting and gathering to survive that we may be. Now I declare, for our continued survival we must write. For should I lose myself again, I can always have these words:

I am enough

I always have been

I always can be.

Through this:

A lovely

Sincerity.

Until eventually,
my frame receives their strength
to grow as bold . . ."

". . . Simply being in an honest pursuit toward truth—a sacred self-reflection . . . Capable of stabilizing Sincere Individuals in their honest pursuit toward truth. To discover oneself completely would be to discover the universe completely—for as we create by relation, so were we created. These conditions appear like they were created for us, for these are the conditions that have made us . . ."

"... We are those who dare to believe we can discover the secrets of the universe, wondering if we but look through life with that lens one day we will and there will be no limit to it. We should all be bold enough to believe we can discover the secrets of the universe. With that lens I believe one day we will, and there will be no limit to it..."

". . . May these words declare our wars and rumors of wars as the breaking of prophecy, no longer to be excused as a fulfillment. In the last days of leadership, We will be lovers of ourselves . . ."

*". . . Seen in the peacemakers of Islam
the wisdom of Rabbis
the sacredness of Saints,
         simmering through all Christianity
I see the Divine
I see the Sincere Individual—
For Sincerity is Divinity."*

A Thank-You

I would love to personally hear your honest review of these excerpts or, in other words, this "prelude" to *Heaven in Earth* which you can send to: themammothsunflower@gmail.com.

For further inquiries or to simply connect, you can also reach out to me at the email above, and be sure to connect with me on Instagram at @benjensen801.

Sincerely, thank you for reading. Thank you for being a part of this one great daring return. Let's do this together.

www.ingramcontent.com/pod-product-compliance
Lightning Source LLC
Chambersburg PA
CBHW020442030426
42337CB00014B/1361